Migraine 84 Success Secrets

84 Most Asked Questions On Migraine

What You Need To Know

Contents

Hallucination - Migraine coma

This sort of delusion is normally accomplished throughout the recuperation as of a unconscious state. The migraine state of unconsciousness may final for up to 2 days, and a state of sadness is occasionally Comorbidity|comorbid. The delusions happen throughout states of complete awareness, and perceptiveness in to the hallucinatory essence of the pictures is conserved. It has been marked that ataxic wounds escort the migraine state of unconsciousness.

Migraine - Epidemiology

Worldwide, migraines influence almost 15% either about one billion folks. It is further commonplace in females at 19% compared to males at 11%. In the United States, about 6% of males and 18% of females get a migraine in a specified annum, with a life span hazard of regarding 18% and 43% correspondingly. In Europe, migraines influence 12–28% of folks at whatever point in their lives with regarding 6–15% of grown-up males and 14–35% of grown-up females getting at minimum one annual. Rates of migraines are somewhat nether in Asia and Africa compared to in Western nations.The Headaches, pp. 238–40 Chronic migraines happen in about one.4 to 2.2% of the populace.

These numbers differ considerably with age: migraines nearly all normally commence amid 15 and 24 annums of age and happen nearly all often in these 35 to 45 annums of age. In kids, about one.7% of 7year olds and 3.9% of these amid seven and 15years have migraines, with the state being somewhat further commonplace in lads beforehand pubescence. During puberty migraines goes further commonplace amid females and this perseveres for the respite of the existance, being 2 periods further commonplace amid aging women compared to masculines. In females migraines short of atmosphere is further commonplace compared to migraines with atmosphere, nevertheless in males the 2 kinds happen with alike incidence.

During perimenopause indications frequently get falling short of a standard beforehand reducing in rigor. While indications settle in regarding 2 thirds of the aging, in amid 3 and 10% they persevere.

Lewis Caroll - Migraine and epilepsy

In his journal for 1880, Dodgson recorded undergoing his foremost chapter of migraine with atmosphere, delineating real precisely the procedure of 'moving fortifications' that are a display of the atmosphere stage of the condition.Wakeling, Edward [http://www.wakeling.demon.co.uk] (Ed.) The Diaries of Lewis Carroll, Vol nine p. 52 Unfortunately there is no clear proof to display if this was his foremost encounter of migraine per se, either if he might have formerly endured the long further commonplace shape of migraine short of atmosphere, though the last one appears nearly all probable, specified the reality that migraine nearly all normally progresses in the teens either first maturity.Migraine and Lewis Carroll; FW Maudie, in The Migraine Periodical, Another shape of migraine atmosphere, Alice in Wonderland condition, has been designated following Dodgson's itty-bitty superwoman, since its display may look like the unexpected size-changes in the publication. Also recognized like micropsia and macropsia, it is a cerebrum state touching the way items are detected by the intellect. For instance, an afflicted individual might guise at a greater article, like a basket ball, and see it like if it were the dimension of a golf ball. Some writers have proposed that Dodgson might have endured as of this sort of atmosphere, and applied it like an stimulation in his work, however there is no proof that he did.

Dodgson as well endured 2 charges in that he missed awareness. He was identified by 3 dissimilar doctors; a Dr. Morshead, Dr. Brooks, and Dr. Stedman, assumed the assault and a resulting assault to be an epileptiform seizure (initially thought to be fainting, however Brooks altered his mind). Some have decided as of this he was a life span sufferer of this state, however there is no proof of this in his Diaries past the analysis of the 2 charges previously alluded to.The Diaries of Lewis Carroll, Vol nine Some writers, in specific Sadi Ranson, have proposed Carroll might have endured as of secular lobe epilepsy in that awareness is not on every relevant occasion totally missed, however changed, and in that the indications imitate numerous of the similar encounters as Alice in Wonderland. Carroll had at minimum one occurrence in that he endured complete loss of awareness and awoke with a blood-stained muzzle, that he recorded in his journal and marked that the chapter left him not understanding him self for pretty at some time later. This assault was identified as perhaps epileptiform and Carroll him self afterward authored of his attacks in the similar journal.

Most of the criterion analytic quizzes of this day were not accessible in the nineteenth era. Recently, Dr Yvonne Hart, adviser brain doctor at the Radcliffe Hospital, Oxford, deemed Dodgson's indications. Her deduction, stated in Jenny Woolf's The Mystery of Lewis Carroll, is that Dodgson real probable had migraine, and might have had epilepsy, however she highlights that she ought to have substantial distrust about creating a analysis of epilepsy short of additional data.

Migraine - Genetics

Studies of twins specify a 34% to 51% hereditary impact of probability to create migraine headaches. This hereditary connection is tougher for migraines with atmosphere compared to for migraines short of atmosphere. A numeral of concrete versions of genetic factors rise the hazard by a not so large to modest quantity.

Single segment of DNA dysfunctionalities that effect in migraines are scarce. One of those is recognized like family hemiplegic migraine, a sort of migraine with atmosphere, that is received in an autosomal authoritative style. Four genetic factors have been presented to be included in family hemiplegic migraine. Three of those genetic factors are included in ion conveyance. The 4th is an axonal protein related with the exocytosis compound. Another hereditary chaos related with migraine is CADASIL condition either cerebral autosomal authoritative arteriopathy with subcortical infarcts and leukoencephalopathy.

Migraines - Medication

Preventive migraine medicines are deemed effectual if they lessen the incidence either rigor of the migraine charges by at minimum 50%. Guidelines are reasonably coherent in grading topiramate, divalproex/sodium valproate, propranolol, and Lopressor as experiencing the biggest layer of proof for First-line treatment|first-line employ. Recommendations concerning success diverse nevertheless for gabapentin. Timolol is as well effectual for migraine deterrence and in decreasing migraine assault incidence and rigor, when frovatriptan is effectual for deterrence of menstrual migraine.

Amitriptyline and venlafaxine are undoubtedly as well effectual. Angiotensin shyness by whichever an angiotensin-converting enzyme inhibitor either angiotonin II sensory receptor adversary might lessen charges. Botox has been noticed to be practical in these with long-lasting migraines however not these with sporadic ones.

Migraine - Triggers

Migraines might be persuaded by precipitates, with whatever informing it like an impact in a smaller group of instances and other ones the major part. Many items have been tagged as precipitates, nevertheless the potency and importance of those connections are unsure. A spark might be ran into up to 24 hours previous to the start of indications.

Migraine - Dietary aspects

Reviews of Dietary precipitates have noticed that proof mainly depends on self-reports and is not meticulous sufficient to show either refute whatever specific precipitates. Regarding concrete representatives there does not emerge to be proof for an result of tyramine on migraine and when monosodium glutamate (MSG) is often announced as a Dietary spark proof does not coherently aid this.

Migraines - Diagnosis

The analysis of a migraine is founded on indications and indications. Neuroimaging quizzes are not required to identify migraine, however might be applied to notice additional triggers of headaches in these whose test and past do not assert a migraine analysis. It is assumed that a considerable numeral of folks with the state stay not diagnosed.

The analysis of migraine short of atmosphere, depending to the International Headache Society, may be produced depending to the ensuing standards, the five, four, 3, 2, one criteria:
* Five either further attacks—for migraine with atmosphere, 2 charges are adequate for analysis.
* Four hours to 3 days in duration
* Two either further of the following:
** Unilateral (affecting fifty per cent the head);
** Pulsating;
** Moderate either grave agony intensity;
** Aggravation by either bringing about evasion of procedure material activity
* One either further of the following:
** Nausea either-or vomiting;
** Sensitivity to either light (photophobia) and sound (phonophobia)

If somebody encounters 2 of the following: photophobia, sickness, either impotence to work either research for a day, the analysis is further probable. In these with 4 out of 5 of the following: pulsating migraine, length of 4–72 hours, agony on one aspect of the head, sickness, either indications that impede with the person's life, the likelihood that this is a migraine is 92%. In these with less compared to 3 of those indications the likelihood is 17%.

Migraines - Pain phase

Classically the migraine is unilateral, throbbing, and modest to grave in strength. It normally appears on slowly and is aggravated by material actions. In further compared to 40% of instances nevertheless the agony might be two-sided, and nape agony is normally related. Bilateral agony is especially commonplace in these whoever have migraines short of an atmosphere. Less normally agony might happen firstly in the back either highest of the head. The agony normally endures four to 72 hours in grown-ups, nevertheless in youthful kids often endures fewer compared to 1hour. The incidence of charges is changeable, as of a limited in a life span to some a 7 days, with the mean being about one a month.

The agony is often escorted by sickness, puking, photophobia|sensitivity to light, phonophobia|sensitivity to sound, osmophobia|sensitivity to smells, exhaustion and irascibility. In a basilar artery|basilar migraine, a migraine with neurological indications associated to the cerebrum shoot either with neurological indications on either aspects of the body, commonplace results contain vertigo (medical)|a feel of the planet spinning, light-headedness, and misunderstanding. Nausea happens in nearly 90% of folks, and puking happens in regarding third. Many consequently pursue a dim and calm area. Other indications might contain blurred apparition, nasal closeness, Delhi belly, recurrent urination, pallor, either sweating. Swelling either tenderness of the scalp might happen as may nape rigor. Associated indications are fewer commonplace in the aging.

Rarely, an atmosphere happens short of a following headache;The Headaches, pp.407–19 this is recognized like an acephalgic migraine either a still migraine. However, it is hard to evaluate the incidence of such instances, since folks whoever do not encounter indications grave sufficient to pursue care, might not realise that whatsoever out of the ordinary is occurring to them, and go it off short of informing whatsoever.

Familial hemiplegic migraine - Treatment/ Management

See the equal part in the Migraine#Treatment|main migraine item.

Patients with FHM are inspired to circumvent doings that might spark their charges. Minor head hurt is a commonplace assault precipitant, thus FHM sufferers ought to circumvent interaction athletics. Acetazolamide either criterion narcotics are frequently applied to handle charges, although these directing to vasoconstriction ought to be shunned expected to the hazard of stroke.

Migraine - Pain

The correct method or means of the head agony that happens throughout a migraine is unidentified. Some proof aids a main part for principal anxious configuration constructions (such as the brainstem and diencephalon) when additional information aid the part accessorial activation (such as by way of the sensual neurons that enclose blood crafts of the head and neck). The prospective applicants crafts include: dura mater|dural arteries, Pia mater|pial arteries and extracranial arteries such like these of the scalp. The part of vasodilatation of the extracranial arteries, in specific, is assumed to be important.

Migraines - Analgesics

Recommended opening care for these with gentle to modest indications are straightforward analgesics such like non-steroidal anti-inflammatory narcotics (NSAIDs) either the amalgamation of paracetamol, acetylsalicylic acidic, and caffein. Several NSAIDs have proof to aid their employ. Ibuprofen has been noticed to supply effectual agony respite in regarding fifty per cent of folks and diclofenac has been noticed effectual.

Aspirin may alleviate modest to grave migraine agony, with an success alike to sumatriptan. Ketorolac is accessible in an intravenous conceptualisation. Paracetamol (also recognized like acetaminophen), whichever only either in amalgamation with metoclopramide, is one other effectual care with a low hazard of unfavorable results. In gestation, paracetamol and metoclopramide are considered secure as are NSAIDs till the 3rd trimester.

Meniere's disease - Migraine

There is an expanded generality of migraine in cases with Ménière's illness, with whatever scientific tests displaying about one 3rd of cases undergoing migraines. An alliance with family past of Vestibular migraine has as well been revealed.

Migraine - History

Trepanation, the intentional drilling of cavities in to a cranium, was experienced as first like seven,000BCE. While occasionally folks outlived, numerous ought to have passed away as of the method expected to contagion. It was assumed to work by way of allowing bad spirits flee. William Harvey suggested Trepanation as a care for migraines in the 17th era.

While numerous handlings for migraines have been endeavored, it was not till 1868 that employ of a material that finally turned out to be effectual started. This material was the fungus ergot as of that ergotamine was separated in 1918. Methysergide was elaborated in 1959 and the foremost triptan, sumatriptan, was elaborated in 1988. During the 20th era with stronger research planning effectual preventive measures were noticed and established.

Migraines

An atmosphere (symptom)|aura is a temporary focal neurological occurrence that happens beforehand either throughout the migraine. Auras emerge slowly over a numeral of minutes and normally final fewer compared to 60minutes. Symptoms may be optical, sensual either engine in essence and numerous folks encounter further compared to one. Visual results happen nearly all frequently; they happen in up to 99% of instances and in further compared to 50% of instances are not escorted by sensual either engine results. Vision disruptions frequently comprise of a scintillating scotoma (an zone of limited change in the area of apparition that flickers and might impede with a person's capacity to peruse either drive). These characteristically commence nearby the centre of apparition and then outspread out to the aspects with zigzagging rules that have been depicted like guising like fortifications either enclosures of a fortress. Usually the rules are in black and white however whatever folks as well perceive tinted rules. Some folks cease to have piece of their area of apparition recognized like hemianopsia when other ones encounter blurring.

Sensory aurae are the second nearly all commonplace type; they happen in 30–40% of folks with auras. Often a understanding of pins-and-needles starts on one aspect in the hand and arm and unfurls to the nose–mouth zone on the similar aspect. Numbness normally happens following the tingling has progressed with a loss of proprioceptive|position feel. Other indications of the atmosphere stage may contain talk either lingo disruptions, vertigo|world spinning, and fewer normally engine difficulties. Motor indications specify that this is a hemiplegic migraine, and frailty frequently endures lengthier compared to one hour dissimilar additional auras. Auditory delusions either false beliefs have as well been depicted.

Biofeedback - Migraine

Sargent, Green, and Walters (1972, 1973) revealed that hand-warming might terminate migraines and that autogenic biofeedback instruction might lessen migraine actions. The first Menninger migraine researches, though methodologically feeble (no pretreatment baselines, command groupings, either arbitrary allotment to conditions), burly affected migraine care.
A 2013 evaluation categorized biofeedback amid the methods that could be of help in the administration of long-lasting migraine.

Migraine - Cause

The fundamental triggers of migraines are unidentified. However, they are assumed to be associated to a mixture of natural and hereditary circumstances. They run in relatives in regarding two-thirds of instances and seldom happen expected to a sole segment of DNA flaw. While migraines were at one point assumed to be further commonplace in these of elevated intellect, this does not emerge to be genuine. A numeral of psychological disorder|psychological states are related including: chief melancholic disorder|depression, nervousness disorder|anxiety, and bipolar disorderThe Headaches, pp. 246–47 as are numerous natural happenings either wikt:trigger|triggers.

Vestibular migraine - Classification

'Benign Paroxysmal positional vertigo' - Migraine is normally related with BPPV, the most commonplace Vestibular chaos in cases offering with giddiness. The 2 might be connected by hereditary circumstances either by vascular harm to the maze.

'Ménière's disease' - There is an expanded generality of migraine in cases with Ménière's illness and migraine guides to a considerable defenselessness of elaborating Ménière's illness. But they may be noted. Ménière's illness might proceed on for days either even annums, when migraines characteristically undertake not final lengthier compared to 24 hours.

'Motion sickness' is further widespread in cases with migraine.

'Psychiatric syndromes' Dizziness and spinning vertigo are the second nearly all commonplace manifestation of alarm charges, and they may as well present as a manifestation of chief sadness. Migraine is a hazard reason for elaborating chief sadness and alarm chaos and vice versa.

Migraine - Alternative therapies

While stylostixis might be effectual, genuine stylostixis is not further effectual compared to fake stylostixis, a exercise wherever needles are put unsystematic. Both have a chance of being further effectual compared to procedure heed, with less unfavorable results compared to preventive medicines. Chiropractic handling, physiotherapy, rub and repose could be as effectual like propranolol either topiramate in the deterrence of migraine headaches; nevertheless, the study had whatever difficulties with collection of methods, practices, procedures and rules. The proof to aid backbone handling is substandard and deficient to aid its employ. There is whatever provisional proof of help for magnesium, Coenzyme Q10|coenzyme Q(10), riboflavin, Vitamin B12|vitamin B(12), and feverfew, though information is restricted and stronger caliber tryouts should be directed to reach further conclusive deductions. Of the alternate medications, Butterbur has the finest proof for its employ.

Migraine - Pathophysiology

Migraines are assumed to be a neurovascular chaos with proof helping its systems beginning inside the cerebrum and then extending to the blood crafts.The Headaches Chp. 29, Pg. 276 Some experimenters sense Neuronal systems play a considerable part, when other ones sense blood crafts play the key part. Others sense either are probable essential. High degrees of the neurotransmitter 5-hydroxytryptamine, as well recognized like 5-hydroxytryptamine, are assumed to be included.

Cardiac fibrosis - Anti-migraine drugs targeted at vasoconstrictive serotonin receptors, which also bind to 5-HT2B receptors

Certain anti-migraine narcotics that are earmarked at 5-hydroxytryptamine receptors as vasoconstrictive representatives, have prolonged been recognized to be related with respiratory hypertension and Raynaud's occurrence (both vasoconstrictive effects), as well like retroperitoneal fibrosis (a fibrotic cell/fibrocyte rapid increase result, thought to be alike to cardiac regulator fibrosis). These contain ergotamine and methysergide. Both narcotics may as well trigger cardiac fibrosis.

Migraine - Research

Calcitonin segment of DNA associated peptides (CGRPs) have been noticed to play a part in the pathogenesis of the agony related with migraine. CGRP sensory receptor adversaries, such like olcegepant and telcagepant, have been looked into either in glass and in scientific researches for the care of migraine. In 2011, Merck halted stage III scientific tryouts for their investigational dope telcagepant. Transcranial magnetized arousal as well exhibits pledge.

Migraine - Aura

Cortical extending sadness either extending sadness of Aristides Leão|Leão is bursts of Neuronal actions pursued by a time of idleness, that is noticed in these with migraines with an atmosphere.The Headaches, Chp. 28, pp. 269–72 There are a numeral of clarifications for its event containing activation of NMDA receptors directing to calcium admitting the cell. After the surge of actions the blood stream to the cerebral cortex in the zone influenced is lessened for 2 to 6 hours. It is assumed that once depolarisation journeys down the base of the cerebrum, neurons that feel agony in the head and nape are precipitated.

Migraine - Medication

Preventive migraine medicines are deemed effectual if they lessen the incidence either rigor of the migraine charges by at minimum 50%. Guidelines are reasonably coherent in grading topiramate, divalproex/sodium valproate, propranolol, and Lopressor as experiencing the biggest layer of proof for First-line treatment|first-line employ. Recommendations concerning success diverse nevertheless for gabapentin. Timolol is as well effectual for migraine deterrence and in decreasing migraine assault incidence and rigor, when frovatriptan is effectual for deterrence of menstrual migraine.

Amitriptyline and venlafaxine are undoubtedly as well effectual. Angiotensin shyness by whichever angiotensin-converting enzyme inhibitor either angiotonin II sensory receptor adversary might lessen charges. Botox has been noticed to be practical in these with long-lasting migraines however not these with sporadic ones.

Familial hemiplegic migraine - FHM4 (1q31)

The ultimate recognized location for FHM charts to the q-arm of chromosome one. There are a numeral of alluring applicant genetic factors in this zone, although no alterations in them have up till now been connected to FHM4.

Migraine - Pain phase

Classically the migraine is unilateral, throbbing, and modest to grave in strength. It normally appears on slowly and is aggravated by material actions. In further compared to 40% of instances nevertheless the agony might be two-sided, and nape agony is normally related. Bilateral agony is especially commonplace in these whoever have migraines short of an atmosphere. Less normally agony might happen firstly in the back either highest of the head. The agony normally endures four to 72 hours in grown-ups nevertheless in youthful kids often endures fewer compared to 1hour. The incidence of charges is changeable, as of a limited in a life span to some a 7 days, with the mean being about one a month.

The agony is often escorted by sickness, puking, photophobia|sensitivity to light,

phonophobia|sensitivity to sound, osmophobia|sensitivity to smells, exhaustion and irascibility. In a basilar artery|basilar migraine, a migraine with neurological indications associated to the cerebrum shoot either with neurological indications on either aspects of the body, commonplace results include: vertigo (medical)|a feel of the planet spinning, light-headedness, and misunderstanding. Nausea happens in nearly 90% of folks, and puking happens in regarding third.
Many consequently pursue a dim and calm area. Other indications might include: blurred apparition, nasal closeness, Delhi belly, recurrent urination, pallor, either sweating. Swelling either tenderness of the scalp might happen as may nape rigor. Associated indications are fewer commonplace in the aging.

Vestibular migraine - Epidemiology

The generality of migraine and vertigo is one.6 periods developed in 200 giddiness health center cases compared to in 200 age- and sex-matched powers as of an Orthopaedic health center. Among the cases with Unclassified either idiopathic vertigo, the generality of migraine was presented to be raised. In one other research, migraine cases announced 2.5 periods further vertigo and as well 2.5 further faint signifies throughout headache-free times compared to the powers.

MAV might happen at whatever age with a female:male proportion of amid one.5 and 5:1. Familial event is not unusual. In nearly all cases, migraine headaches start earliest in life compared to MAV with annums of headache-free times beforehand MAV presents.

In a journal research, the 1-month generality of MAV was 16%, incidence of MAV was developed and length lengthier on days with migraine, and MAV was a hazard reason for co-morbid nervousness.

Migraines - Prevention

Preventive handlings of migraines contain medicines, nourishing complements, way of life changes, and operation. Prevention is suggested in these whoever have headaches further compared to 2 days a 7 days, can't endure the medicines applied to handle severe charges, either these with grave charges that are not effortlessly managed.

The objective is to lessen the incidence, distressingness, either-or length of migraines, and to rise the success of unsuccessful treatment. Another cause for deterrence is to circumvent drug overutilisation migraine. This is a commonplace difficulty and may effect in long-lasting everyday migraine.

Migraines - Devices and surgery

Medical implements, such like biofeedback and neurostimulators, have whatever benefits in migraine deterrence, mostly once commonplace anti-migraine medicines are contraindicated either in case of drug overutilisation. Biofeedback assists folks be aware of whatever physical variables thus like to command them and attempt to relax and might be effectual for migraine care. Neurostimulation utilizes implantable neurostimulators alike to Pacemakers for the care of unmanageable long-lasting migraines with inspiring outcomes for grave instances. A transcutaneous electronic nervus arousal implement is accepted in the United States for the deterrence of migraines. Migraine operation, that includes decompressing of definite neurons about the head and nape, might be an choice in definite folks whoever do not better with medicines.

Migraine - Physiological aspects

Common precipitates stated are pressure, hungriness, and exhaustion (these similarly give to pressure headaches). Migraines are further probable to happen about menses. Other hormonal effects, such like menarche, verbal birth control employ, gestation, perimenopause, and menopause, as well play a part. These hormonal effects appear to play a considerable part in migraine short of atmosphere. Migraines characteristically undertake not happen throughout the second trimester|second and 3rd trimesters either ensuing menopause.

Neurostimulation - Migraine Therapy

The Reed Procedure, introduced by Dallas-based anesthetist Dr. Kenneth Reed, had elaborated a to a minimal degree invasive method wherever neurostimulation guides are inserted under the epidermis and neighboring to the sections of agony providing gentle electronic pulses to the neurons. The electronic pulses substitute the understanding of agony with a tingling either massaging impression, decreasing either removing the demand for agony drug in cases whoever are applicants for this care.

Although the Reed Procedure is not at the moment FDA accepted, backbone string arousal (SCS) utilizes the similar technics and was accepted by the FDA in 1989. SCS is at the moment a normal care choice for cases with long-lasting agony in their back either-or arms or legs whoever have not noticed agony respite as of different handlings. Neurostimulation for head agony was given CE Mark acceptance for employ in Europe in September 2011.

Migraine - Postdrome

The results of migraine might persevere for whatever days following the principal migraine has ended; this is named the migraine postdrome. Many outline a aching understanding in the zone wherever the migraine was, and whatever outline afflicted considering for a limited days following the migraine has progressed. The patient might sense exhausted either hung over and have head agony, perceptive problems, gastrointestinal indications, temper amends, and frailty. According to one synopsis, Some folks sense unusually reinvigorated either Euphoric following an assault, while other ones note sadness and unease.

Zonisamide - Migraines

Zonisamide has been learned for and applied like a migraine preventive drug, and has as well been presented to be effectual in whatever instances of neuropathic agony.

Migraine - Environmental aspects

A evaluation on prospective precipitates in the inside and alfresco ecosystem decided the altogether proof was of substandard caliber, however however proposed folks with migraines get whatever preemptive actions associated to inside air caliber and illumination.

Familial hemiplegic migraine - Epidemiology

Migraine its normal self is a real commonplace chaos, happening in 15–20% of the populace. Hemiplegic migraine, be it family either impulsive, is fewer widespread, zero.01% generality depending to one outline. Women are 3 periods further probable to be influenced compared to masculines.

Migraines - Pain

The correct method or means of the head agony that happens throughout a migraine is unidentified. Some proof aids a main part for principal anxious configuration constructions (such as the brainstem and diencephalon) when additional information aid the part of accessorial activation (such as by way of the sensual neurons that enclose blood crafts of the head and neck). The prospective applicant crafts contain dura mater|dural arteries, Pia mater|pial arteries and extracranial arteries such like these of the scalp. The part of vasodilatation of the extracranial arteries, in specific, is assumed to be important.

Migraine - Differential diagnosis

Other states that may trigger alike indications to a migraine migraine include: secular arteritis, group headaches, severe glaucoma, meningitis and subarachnoid bleeding. Temporal arteritis characteristically happens in folks over 50 annums aged and gives with tenderness over the Temple (anatomy)|temple, group headaches gives with biased muzzle closeness, tears and grave agony about the revolves, severe glaucoma is related with apparition difficulties, meningitis with fevers, and subaracchnoid bleeding with a real speedy start. Tension headaches characteristically happen on either aspects, are not hammering, and are fewer incapacitating.

Those with steady headaches that encounter standards for migraines ought to not obtain Neuroimaging to guise for different intracranial illness.

*

*

*

* This needs that additional about discoveries such like papilledema (swelling of the ocular disc) are not present. People with migraines are not at an expanded hazard of experiencing one other trigger for grave headaches.

Vestibular migraine - Diagnosis

MAV is not acknowledged a clearly different analytic being. Lembert and Neuhauser suggest standards for settled and likely migraine-associated vertigo.

A analysis of settled migraine-associated vertigo contains a instance past of:
*episodic Vestibular indications of at minimum modest severity;
*current either foregoing past of migraine depending to the 2004 International Classification of Headache Disorders;
*one of the ensuing migrainous indications throughout 2 either further charges of vertigo: migrainous migraine, photophobia, acousticophobia, atmosphere (symptom)|visual either different auras; and
*other triggers ruled out by suitable examinations.

A analysis of likely migraine-associated vertigo contains a instance past of sporadic Vestibular indications of at minimum modest rigor and one of the following:
*current either foregoing past of migraine depending to the 2004 International Classification of Headache Disorders;
*migrainous indications throughout Vestibular symptoms;
*migraine precipitants of vertigo in further compared to 50% of charges, such like

nourishment sensitivity|food precipitates, slumber anomalies, either hormonal change;
*response to migraine medicines in further compared to 50% of attacks; and
*other triggers ruled out by suitable examinations.

Note that, in either of the overhead standards, migraine is not needed to create the analysis of migraine-associated vertigo.

They append that, in cases with a straightforward past, no Vestibular quizzes are needed. Other past standards that are obliging in creating the analysis of migraine-associated vertigo are vertiginous indications all over the patient's whole life, a prolonged past of motion sensitivity, responsiveness to natural incentives, Illusions of motion of the ecosystem, and vertigo that wakes up the patient.

Migraines - Postdrome

The results of migraine might persevere for whatever days following the principal migraine has ended; this is named the migraine postdrome. Many outline a aching understanding in the zone wherever the migraine was, and whatever outline afflicted considering for a limited days following the migraine has progressed. The patient might sense exhausted either hung over and have head agony, perceptive problems, gastrointestinal indications, temper amends, and frailty. According to one synopsis, Some folks sense unusually reinvigorated either Euphoric following an assault, while other ones note sadness and unease. For whatever single human beings this may differ every one time.

Brain disease - Migraine

A long-lasting, frequently incapacitating neurological chaos distinguished by repeated modest to grave headaches, frequently in alliance with a numeral of autonomic anxious configuration indications.

ATC code N02 - N02CX Other antimigraine preparations

:N02CX01 Pizotifen
:N02CX02 Clonidine
:N02CX03 Iprazochrome
:N02CX05 Dimetotiazine
:N02CX06 Oxetorone

Migraines - Research

Calcitonin segment of DNA associated peptides (CGRPs) have been noticed to play a part in the pathogenesis of the agony related with migraine. CGRP sensory receptor adversaries, such like olcegepant and telcagepant, have been looked into either in glass and in scientific researches for the care of migraine. In 2011, Merck halted stage III scientific tryouts for their investigational dope telcagepant. Transcranial magnetized arousal exhibits pledge as has transcutaneous supraorbital nervus arousal.

Retinal migraine

'Retinal migraine' (also recognized like 'ophthalmic migraine', 'visual migraine' and 'ocular migraine') is a retinal illness frequently escorted by migraine migraine and characteristically influences solely one eye.[http://www.eugeneeyecare.com/conditions/Ophthalmic_Migraine.html ophthalmic migraine] It is triggered by an infarction either vascular spasm in either beyond the influenced eye.

The specifications retinal migraine and visual migraine are frequently puzzled with an unusual state in the cerebrum (cortical extending depression) that might trigger alike indications such like scintillating scotoma touching apparition in either senses, as well related with migraine headaches.

Migraines - Cause

The fundamental triggers of migraines are unidentified. However, they are assumed to be associated to a mixture of natural and hereditary circumstances. They run in relatives in regarding two-thirds of instances and seldom happen expected to a sole segment of DNA flaw. While migraines were at one point assumed to be further commonplace in these of elevated intellect, this does not emerge to be genuine. A numeral of psychological disorder|psychological states are related, containing chief melancholic disorder|depression, nervousness disorder|anxiety, and bipolar chaos,The Headaches, pp. 246–47 as are numerous natural happenings either wikt:trigger|triggers.

Migraine - Prognosis

Long period prognosis in folks with migraines is changeable. Most folks with migraines have times of missed efficiency expected to their illness nevertheless characteristically the state is reasonably gentle and is not related with an expanded hazard of demise. There are 4 principal models to the disease: indications may settle totally, indications may resume however come to be slowly fewer with time, indications might resume at the similar incidence and rigor, either charges might come to be falling short of a standard and further recurrent.

Migraines with atmosphere emerge to be a hazard reason for ischemic stroke dualling the hazard. Being a youthful grown-up, being feminine, utilizing hormonal birth control, and smoking additional upsurges this hazard. There as well shows to be an alliance with cervical arterial anatomy. Migraines short of atmosphere do not emerge to be a reason. The connection with heart difficulties is inconclusive with a sole research helping an alliance. Overall nevertheless migraines do not emerge to rise the hazard of demise as of stroke either heart illness. Preventative treatment of migraines in these with migraines with auras might stop related strokes.

Botulinum toxin A - Chronic migraine

Onabotulinumtoxin A (trade designation Botox) experienced FDA acceptance for care of long-lasting migraines on October 15, 2010. The poison is introduced in to the head and nape to handle those long-lasting headaches. Approval pursued proof offered to the organization as of 2 researches financed by Allergan, Inc. Displaying a real small advancement in occurrence of long-lasting migraines for migraine sufferers experiencing the Botox care.

Since additionally, some randomized command tryouts have presented botulinum poison sort A to better migraine indications and caliber of life once applied prophylactically for cases with long-lasting migraine whoever display migraine attributes coherent with: force detected as of external origin, smaller whole length of long-lasting migraines (30 years), detoxification of cases with coexisting long-lasting everyday migraine expected to drug overutilisation, and no current past of different preemptive migraine medicines.

Familial hemiplegic migraine - FHM3 (SCN1A)

The ultimate recognized Locus (genetics)|locus FHM3 is the SCN1A segment of DNA, that encodes a Na delivery method α subunit. The solely research thus long that has noticed alterations in this segment of DNA ascertained the similar Q1489K alteration in 3 of 20 relatives (15%) with 11 additional kindreds (55%) previously experiencing alterations in CACNA1A either ATP1A2. This alteration is found in a extremely preserved area of an intracellular circle linking areas 3 and 4. This alteration outcomes in a considerably hastened (2–4 fold) recuperation as of inactivation contrasted to wild-type. As this delivery method is essential for activity prospective propagation in nerve cells, it is anticipated that the Q1489K distorted outcomes in hyperexcitable nerve cells.

Vestibular migraine - Signs and symptoms

Vertigo is a therapeutically acknowledged expression for the manifestation of Vestibular configuration disruption. It might contain a understanding of gyration either illusory sensations of motion either either. The common expression giddiness is applied by nonmedical folks for these indications however frequently alludes to a understanding of light-headedness, silliness, sleepiness, either faintness, altogether of that ought to be distinguished as of genuine vertigo, eversince the last one indications could have additional triggers.

Motion illness happens further often in migraine cases (30-50%) compared to in powers. Benign Paroxysmal vertigo of youth is an illustration of migraine-associated vertigo in that migraine does not frequently happen. Migraine#Classification|Basilar migraine comprises of 2 either further indications (vertigo, tinnitus, lessened perceiving, ataxia, Dysarthria, optical indications in either hemifields either either senses, diplopia, two-sided paresthesias, paresis, lessened awareness either-or loss of consciousness) pursued by throbbing migraine. Auditory indications are scarce. However, a research presented a varying low-tone sensorineural perceiving loss in further compared to 50% of cases with BAM with a obvious shift in perceiving simply beforehand the start of a migraine migraine. The charges of vertigo are normally simultaneous with the migraine and the kin past is normally optimistic. The pathologist should command out: Transient ischemic attack|TIAs, and Paroxysmal Vestibular chaos escorted by migraine.

There is as well a family vestibulopathy, family gentle repeated vertigo (fBRV), wherever chapters of vertigo happen with either short of migraine migraine. Testing might show heartfelt Vestibular loss. The condition replies to acetazolamide. Familial hemiplegic migraine (FHM) has been connected to alterations in the calcium delivery method segment of DNA. (Ophoff et al. 1966 cf. Lempert et al.)

Antimigraine

An 'antimigraine' dope is a drug designed to lessen the results either strength of migraine migraine.

Examples contain triptans[http://pharmamotion.com.ar/serotonin-5ht-receptors-agonists-antagonist/ pharmamotion.com /refref name=pmid16549032/ref and ergoline|ergot alkaloids such like methysergide.

Antimigraine medicines are categorized under N02C in the Anatomical Therapeutic Chemical Classification System

Migraine - Prevention

Preventive handlings of migraines include: medicines, nourishing complements, way of life changes, and operation. Prevention is suggested in these whoever have headaches further compared to 2 days a 7 days, can't endure the medicines applied to handle severe charges, either these with grave charges that are not effortlessly managed.

The objective is to lessen the incidence, distressingness, either-or length of migraines, and to rise the success of unsuccessful treatment. Another cause for deterrence is to circumvent drug overutilisation migraine. This is a commonplace difficulty and may effect in long-lasting everyday migraine.

Migraines - Differential diagnosis

Other states that may trigger alike indications to a migraine migraine contain secular arteritis, group headaches, severe glaucoma, meningitis and subarachnoid bleeding. Temporal arteritis characteristically happens in folks over 50 annums aged and gives with tenderness over the Temple (anatomy)|temple, group headaches gives with biased muzzle closeness, tears and grave agony about the Orbit (anatomy)|orbits, severe glaucoma is related with apparition difficulties, meningitis with fevers, and subaracchnoid bleeding with a real speedy start. Tension headaches characteristically happen on either aspects, are not hammering, and are fewer incapacitating.

Those with steady headaches that encounter standards for migraines ought to not obtain Neuroimaging to guise for different intracranial illness.

*

*

*

* This needs that additional about discoveries such like papilledema (swelling of the ocular disc) are not present. People with migraines are not at an expanded hazard of experiencing one other trigger for grave headaches.

Migraine - Diagnosis

The analysis of a migraine is founded on indications and indications. Neuroimaging quizzes are not required to identify migraine, however might be applied to notice additional triggers of headaches in these whose test and past do not assert a migraine analysis. It is assumed that a considerable numeral of folks with the state have not been identified.

The analysis of migraine short of atmosphere, depending to the International Headache Society, may be produced depending to the ensuing standards, the five, four, 3, 2, one criteria:
* Five either further attacks—for migraine with atmosphere, 2 charges are adequate for analysis.
* Four hours to 3 days in duration
* Two either further of the following:
** Unilateral (affecting fifty per cent the head);
** Pulsating;
** Moderate either grave agony intensity;
** Aggravation by either bringing about evasion of procedure material activity
* One either further of the following:
** Nausea either-or vomiting;
** Sensitivity to either light (photophobia) and sound (phonophobia)

If somebody encounters 2 of the following: photophobia, sickness, either impotence to work / research for a day the analysis is further probable. In these with 4 out of 5 of the following: pulsating migraine, length of 4–72 hours, agony on one aspect of the head, sickness, either indications that impede with the person's life, the likelihood that this is a migraine is 92%. In these with fewer compared to 3 of those indications the likelihood is 17%.

Retinal migraine - Symptoms

Retinal migraine is related with temporary monocular optical loss (scotoma) in one eye enduring fewer compared to one hour. During whatever chapters, the optical loss might happen with no migraine and at additional periods throbbing migraine on the similar aspect of the head as the optical loss might happen, escorted by grave light responsiveness either-or sickness. Visual loss inclines to influence the whole monocular optical area of one eye, not either senses.[http://natural-headache-remedies.blogspot.com/ Retinal Migraine by Todd Troost] After every one chapter, usual apparition returns.

It might be hard to peruse and hazardous to drive a means of transport when retinal migraine indications are present.

Retinal migraine is a dissimilar illness compared to scintillating scotoma, that is a optical oddity triggered by extending sadness in the occipital cortex, at the back of the cerebrum, not in the senses nor whatever part of that.[http://imigraine.net/migraine/genetics.html Genetics in Migraine] Unlike retinal migraine, such a scintillating atmosphere influences apparition as of either senses, and sufferers might perceive flashes of light; zigzagging patterns; imperceptive spots; and shimmering spots either stars. In juxtaposition, retinal migraine includes redone attacks of provisional faded apparition either sightlessness in one eye.[http://www.ohiohealth.com/blank.cfm?print=yesid=6action=detailref=4024 Ocular migraine]

Transient global amnesia - Migraine

A past of migraine is a statistically important hazard reason recognized in the health written works. When contrasting TGA cases with usual command subjects... the solely reason notably related with an expanded hazard for TGA was migraine. 14% of folks with TGA had a past of migraine in one research, and about a 3rd of the contributors in one other scientific research announced such a past.

However, migraine does not emerge to happen concurrently with TGA nor service like a causing happening. Headache often happens throughout TGA, as does sickness, either indications frequently related with migraine, however it shows that those do not specify migraine in cases throughout a TGA happening. The link stays abstract, and muddied additional by a absence of consensus regarding the meaning of migraine its normal self, and by the dissimilarities in age, sex, and mental attributes of migraine sufferers once contrasted to these factors in the TGA cohort.

Familial hemiplegic migraine - Prevention/Screening

Prenatal viewing is not characteristically completed for FHM, nevertheless it might be accomplished if solicited. As penetrance is elevated, single human beings noticed to take alterations ought to be anticipated to create indications of FHM at whatever point in life.

Vestibular migraine - Pathophysiology

The pathophysiology of MAV is not totally understood; either principal and accessorial faults have been noticed.

Migraines - Abdominal migraine

The analysis of stomach migraines is contentious. Some proof designates that repeated chapters of stomach agony in the nonappearance of a migraine might be a sort of migraine either are at minimum a forerunner to migraines. These chapters of agony might either might not come after a migraine-like prodroma and characteristically final minutes to hours. They frequently happen in these with whichever a private either kin past of distinctive migraines. Other syndromes that are assumed to be precursors contain cyclical puking condition and gentle Paroxysmal vertigo of youth.

Hemoencephalography - Migraines

Research with PIR has concentrated nearly solely on easing pressure headaches and migraines. A 4 annum research of 100 long-lasting migraine sufferers noticed that following as limited like 6 30-minute instruction meetings, 90% of cases announced important advancements with their migraines. Another research directed rolled into one the biofeedback actions of EEG, hemoencephalography and air current handwarming throughout thrice once a week meetings for 14 months. 70% of sufferers saw a 50% either further decrease in their migraines ensuing rolled into one neurotherapy and dope care, as against to 50% experiencing solely customary dope treatment.Stokes, D.A. Lappin, M.S.. (2010). Neurofeedback and biofeedback with 37 migraineurs: a scientific result research. Behavioral and Brain Functions, 6(9), 1–10.

Migraine - Devices and surgery

Medical implements, such like biofeedback and neurostimulators, have whatever benefits in migraine deterrence, mostly once commonplace anti-migraine medicines are contraindicated either in case of drug overutilisation. Biofeedback assists folks be aware of whatever physical variables thus like to command them and attempt to relax and might be effectual for migraine care. Neurostimulation utilizes implantable neurostimulators alike to Pacemakers for the care of unmanageable long-lasting migraines with inspiring outcomes for grave instances. Migraine operation, that includes decompressing of definite neurons about the head and nape, might be an choice in definite folks whoever do not better with medicines.

Migraines - Dietary aspects

Reviews of Dietary precipitates have noticed that proof mainly depends on self-reports and is not meticulous sufficient to show either refute whatever specific precipitates. Regarding concrete representatives there does not emerge to be proof for an result of tyramine on migraine, and when monosodium glutamate (MSG) is often announced as a Dietary spark, proof does not coherently aid this.

Retinal migraine - Treatment

Treatment relies on recognizing conduct that precipitates migraine such like pressure, slumber loss, jumped meals, nourishment sensitivities, either concrete doings. Medicines applied to handle retinal migraines contain aspirin, additional NSAIDS, and medications that lessen elevated blood force.

Retinal migraine - Diagnosis

The health examination ought to command out whatever fundamental triggers, such like blood lump, stroke, pituitary malignancy, either disconnected retina. A usual retina examination is coherent with retinal migraine.[http://headaches.about.com/lw/Health-Medicine/Conditions-and-diseases/Retinal-Ocular-Migraines.htm Retinal (Ocular) Migraines]

Familial hemiplegic migraine - FHM2 (ATP1A2)

The second subtype of family hemiplegic migraine, FHM2, is triggered by alterations in the segment of DNA ATP1A2 that encodes a Na+/K+-ATPase|/-ATPase. This /-ATPase is deeply communicated in astrocytes and assists to set and preserve their turnaround prospective. There are 29 recognized alterations in this segment of DNA related with FHM2, Table 2, numerous agglomerating in the great intracellular circle amid membrane-spanning sections four and five, Figure one. 12 of those alterations have been learned by articulation in model cells. All but one have presented whichever perfect loss of purpose either further compound reduces in ATPase actions either potassium responsiveness. Astrocytes airing those distorted Ion transporter|ion pumps must have a lot developed lying pissibilities and are assumed to head to illness via a badly comprehended method or means.

Acupuncture - Headaches and migraines

A 2012 evaluation noticed that stylostixis has revealed help for the care of headaches, however that protection required to be further completely recorded in line to create whatever forceful suggestions in aid of its employ. A 2009 Cochrane evaluation of the employ of stylostixis for migraine prophylaxis care decided that genuine stylostixis was no further effectual compared to fake stylostixis, however genuine stylostixis emerged to be as effectual like, either perhaps further effectual compared to procedure heed in the care of migraines, with less unfavorable results compared to prophylactic dope care. The similar evaluation declared that the concrete details selected to pointer might be of restricted significance. A 2009 Cochrane evaluation noticed deficient proof to aid stylostixis for tension-type headaches. The similar evaluation noticed proof that proposed that stylostixis could be deemed a obliging non-pharmacological tactic for recurrent sporadic either long-lasting tension-type migraine.

Migraine - Management

There are 3 principal facets of treatment: spark evasion, severe indicative command, and pharmacological deterrence. Medications are further effectual if applied earliest in an assault. The recurrent employ of medicines might effect in drug overutilisation migraine, in that the headaches come to be further grave and further recurrent. This might happen with triptans, ergotamines, and analgesics, particularly drugs analgesics. Due to those bothers straightforward analgesics are suggested to be applied fewer compared to 3 days per 7 days at nearly all.

Migraines - Aura

Cortical extending sadness, either extending sadness depending to Aristides Leão|Leão, is bursts of Neuronal actions pursued by a time of idleness, that is noticed in these with migraines with an atmosphere.The Headaches, Chp. 28, pp. 269–72 There are a numeral of clarifications for its event containing activation of NMDA receptors directing to calcium admitting the cell. After the surge of actions the blood stream to the cerebral cortex in the zone influenced is lessened for 2 to 6 hours. It is assumed that once depolarisation journeys down the base of the cerebrum, neurons that feel agony in the head and nape are precipitated.

Central nervous system disease - Migraine

A long-lasting frequently incapacitating neurological chaos distinguished by repeated modest to grave headaches frequently in alliance with a numeral of autonomic anxious configuration indications.

Migraine - Classification

Migraines were foremost in an all-inclusive manner categorized in 1988.The Headaches, Pg 232-233 The International Headache Society nearly all not long ago upgraded their categorization of headaches in 2004. According to this categorization migraines are main headaches alongside with tension-type headaches and group headaches, amid other ones.

Migraines are split in to 7 subclasses (some of that contain additional subdivisions):

* Migraine short of atmosphere, either commonplace migraine, includes migraine headaches that are not escorted by an aura
* Migraine with atmosphere, either timeless migraine, normally includes migraine headaches escorted by an atmosphere. Less normally, an atmosphere may happen short of a migraine, either with a nonmigraine migraine. Two additional diversities are family hemiplegic migraine and occasional hemiplegic migraine, in that a individual has migraines with atmosphere and with subsequent engine frailty. If a close comparative has had the similar state, it is named family, else it is named occasional. Another diversity is basilar-type migraine, wherever a migraine and atmosphere are escorted by dysarthria|difficulty talking, Vertigo (medical)|world spinning, tinnitus|ringing in ears, either a numeral of different brainstem-related indications, however not engine frailty. This sort was originally assumed to be expected to spasms of the basilar arterial, the arterial that furnishes the brainstem.
* Childhood periodical syndromes that are normally precursors of migraine contain cyclical puking syndrome|cyclical puking (occasional extreme times of vomiting), stomach migraine (abdominal agony, normally escorted by nausea), and gentle Paroxysmal vertigo of youth (occasional charges of vertigo).
* Retinal migraine includes migraine headaches escorted by optical disruptions either even provisional sightlessness in one eye.
* Complications of migraine report migraine headaches either-or auras that are unusually prolonged either unusually recurrent, either related with a seizure either cerebrum wound.
* Probable migraine explains states that have whatever attributes of migraines, however wherever there is not sufficient proof to identify it like a migraine with confidence (in the occurrence of simultaneous drug overuse).
* Chronic migraine is a difficulty of migraines, and is a migraine that attains analytic standards for migraine migraine and happens for a considerable time intermission. Specifically, considerable either identical to 15 days/month for lengthier compared to 3 months.

Migraine - Abdominal migraine

The analysis of stomach migraines is contentious. Some proof designates that repeated chapters of stomach agony in the nonappearance of a migraine might be a sort of migraine either are at minimum a forerunner to migraines. These chapters of agony might either might not come after a migraine like prodroma and characteristically final minutes to hours. They frequently happen in these with whichever a private either kin past of distinctive migraines. Other syndromes that are assumed to be precursors include: cyclical puking condition and gentle Paroxysmal vertigo of youth.

Migraine - Analgesics

Recommended opening care for these with gentle to modest indications are straightforward analgesics such like non-steroidal anti-inflammatory narcotics (NSAIDs) either the amalgamation of paracetamol, acetylsalicylic acidic, and caffein. A numeral of NSAIDs have proof to aid their employ. Ibuprofen has been noticed to supply effectual agony respite in regarding fifty per cent of folks and diclofenac has been noticed effectual.

Aspirin may alleviate modest to grave migraine agony, with an success alike to sumatriptan. Ketorolac is accessible in an intravenous conceptualisation. Paracetamol (also recognized like acetaminophen), whichever only either in amalgamation with metoclopramide, is one other effectual care with a low hazard of unfavorable results. In gestation, paracetamol and metoclopramide are considered secure as are NSAIDs till the 3rd trimester.

Methylergometrine - Migraine

Methylergometrine is occasionally applied aimed at either deterrence and severe care of migraine. It is an energetic metabolite of methysergide.

Vestibular migraine - Treatment

Treatment of migraine-associated vertigo is the similar like the care for migraine in common.

Vestibular migraine

'Migraine-associated vertigo' (MAV) is Vertigo (medical)|vertigo related with a migraine, whichever like a manifestation of migraine either like a associated but neurological disorder; once referenced to like a illness unto its normal self, it is as well named 'vestibular migraine', 'migrainous vertigo', either 'migraine-related vestibulopathy'.

A 2010 outline as of the University of British Columbia issued in the periodical Headache (journal)|Headache indicated that it ...is upcoming as a well-liked analysis for cases with repeated vertigo. Even although whatever writers trust that 'migraine related vertigo,' is not the one nor the other clinically nor Biologically credible as a migraine variation. Epidemiological researches leave no distrust that there is a forceful link amid vertigo and migraine.

Migraine - Society and culture

Migraines are a important origin of either health outlays and missed efficiency. It has been approximated that they are the most expensive neurological chaos in the European Community, charging further compared to €27 billion per annum. In the United States straight outlays have been approximated at $17billion, Nearly a tenth of this outlay is expected to the outlay of triptans. Containing $15 billion in circuitous outlays, of that missed work is the largest part. In these whoever do be at work with a migraine, success is lessened by about a 3rd. Negative effects as well often happen for a person's kin.

International Classification of Headache Disorders - ICHD 1, ICD10 G43: Migraine

:Migraine short of aura
:Migraine with aura
:Childhood periodical syndromes that are normally precursors of migraine
:Retinal migraine
:Complications of migraine
:Migraine-triggered seizure
:Probable migraine

Retinal migraine - Prognosis

In common, the prognosis for retinal migraine is alike to that of migraine migraine with distinctive atmosphere. As the genuine occurrence of retinal migraine is unidentified, it is unsure if there is a developed occurrence of enduring neuroretinal accident. The optical area information proposes that there is a developed occurrence of finish arteriolar dispersion infarction and a developed occurrence of enduring optical area faults in retinal migraine compared to in clinically apparent cerebral infarctions in migraine with atmosphere. One research proposes that further compared to fifty per cent of announced repeated instances of retinal migraine afterward accomplished enduring optical loss in that eye as of infarcts. An infarction in the retina, nevertheless, is normally obvious to the patient.

Migraine - Ergotamines

Ergotamine and dihydroergotamine are aged medicines nevertheless prescribed for migraines, the last one in nasal shower and injectable forms. They emerge similarly effectual to the triptans, are fewer costly, and encounter unfavorable results that characteristically are gentle. In the most incapacitating instances, such like these with condition migrainosus, they emerge to be the most effectual care choice.

Migraines - Alternative therapies

While stylostixis might be effectual, genuine stylostixis is not further effectual compared to fake stylostixis, a exercise wherever needles are put unsystematic. Both have a chance of being further effectual compared to procedure heed, with less unfavorable results compared to preventive medicines. Chiropractic handling, physiotherapy, rub and repose could be as effectual like propranolol either topiramate in the deterrence of migraine headaches; nevertheless, the study had whatever difficulties with collection of methods, practices, procedures and rules. The proof to aid backbone handling is substandard and deficient to aid its employ. Of the alternate medications, Butterbur has the finest proof for its employ.

Migraine

An atmosphere (symptom)|aura is a temporary focal neurological occurrence that happens beforehand either throughout the migraine. They emerge slowly over a numeral of minutes and normally final less compared to 60minutes. Symptoms may be optical, sensual either engine in essence and numerous folks encounter further compared to one. Visual results happen nearly all frequently; they happen in up to 99% of instances and in further compared to 50% of instances are not escorted by sensual either engine results. Vision disruptions frequently comprise of a scintillating scotoma (an zone of limited change in the area of apparition that flickers and might impede with a person's capacity to peruse either drive.) These characteristically commence nearby the centre of apparition and then outspread out to the aspects with zigzagging rules that have been depicted like guising like fortifications either enclosures of a fortress. Usually the rules are in black and white however whatever folks as well perceive tinted rules. Some folks cease to have piece of their area of apparition recognized like hemianopsia when other ones encounter blurring.

Sensory aurae are the second nearly all commonplace type; they happen in 30–40% of folks with auras. Often a understanding of pins-and-needles starts on one aspect in the hand and arm and unfurls to the nose-mouth zone on the similar aspect. Numbness normally happens following the tingling has progressed with a loss of proprioceptive|position feel. Other indications of the atmosphere stage may include: talk either lingo disruptions, vertigo|world spinning, and fewer normally engine difficulties. Motor indications specify that this is a hemiplegic migraine, and frailty frequently endures lengthier compared to one hour dissimilar additional auras.

An atmosphere seldom happens short of a following migraine,The Headaches, pp.407–19 recognized like a still migraine. However, it is hard to evaluate the incidence of such instances, since cases whoever do not encounter indications grave sufficient to drive them to pursue care, might not realise that whatsoever out of the ordinary is occurring to them, and go it off short of informing whatsoever.

Migraine - Triptans

Triptans such like sumatriptan are effectual for either agony and sickness in up to 75% of folks. They are the originally suggested handlings for these with modest to grave agony either these with gentler indications whoever do not answer to straightforward analgesics. The dissimilar forms accessible contain verbal, injectable, nasal shower, and verbal dissolving notepads. In common, altogether the triptans emerge similarly effectual, with alike aspect results. However, single human beings might answer stronger to concrete ones. Most aspect results are gentle, such like flushing; nevertheless, scarce instances of myocardial ischaemia have happened. They are consequently not suggested for folks with circulatory illness, whoever have had a stroke, either have migraines that are escorted by neurological difficulties. In extension, triptans ought to be prescribed with carefulness for these with hazard circumstances for vascular illness. While with reference to past events not suggested in these with basilar migraines there is no concrete proof of damage as of their employ in this populace to aid this carefulness. They are not addicting, however might trigger drug overutilisation headaches if applied further compared to ten days per month.

Phantosmia - Migraines

In 2011 Coleman, Grosberg and Robbins did a instance research on cases with olfactory delusions and different main migraine dysfunctionalities. In their 30 months prolonged research, the generality rates for Phantosmia turned out to be a low like zero.66%.

In their discoveries, it was noticed that a distinctive delusion time was of 5–60 minutes, happened whichever beforehand either with the start of head agony, and characteristically comprised of an disagreeable scent. It was as well marked that Phantosmia happens nearly all normally amid females experiencing a migraine objection.Coleman, E. R., Grosberg, B. M., Robbins, M. S. (2011). Olfactory delusions in main migraine disorders: Case serials and written works evaluation. Cephalalgia,

31(14), 1477-1489. In their research, prophylactic treatment for headaches aided remedy Phantosmia in nearly all of the cases.

This detecting is coherent with the discoveries of Schreiber and Calvert in 1986 that as well alluded to the olfactory delusions beforehand the event of a migraine assault in 4 of their topics.Schrieber, A. O., Calvert, P. C. (1986). Migrainous olfactory delusions. Headache: The Journal of Head and Face Pain, 26(10), 513-514

Vertigo (medical) - Vestibular migraine

Vestibular migraine is the alliance of vertigo and migraines and is one of the most commonplace triggers of repeated, impulsive chapters of vertigo. The aetiology of Vestibular migraines is right now unclear; nevertheless, one suggested trigger is that the arousal of the trigeminal nervus guides to nystagmus in single human beings hurting as of migraines. Other proposed triggers of Vestibular migraines contain the following: unilateral Neuronal unstableness of the Vestibular nervus, idiopathic irregular activation of the Vestibular centers in the brainstem, and vasospasm of the blood crafts providing the maze either principal Vestibular trails ensuing in ischaemia to those constructions. Vestibular migraines are approximated to influence 1-3% of the common populace and might influence 10% of migraine cases. Additionally, Vestibular migraines incline to happen further frequently in females and seldom influence single human beings following the 6th period of 10 years of life.

Migraine - Other

Intravenous metoclopramide either intranasal Xylocaine are different prospective choices. Metoclopramide is the suggested care for these whoever present to the crisis division. A sole measure of intravenous dexamethasone, once appended to normal care of a migraine assault, is related with a 26% reduce in migraine return in the ensuing 72 hours. Spinal handling for treating an continuing migraine migraine is not maintained by proof. It is suggested that opioids and barbiturates not be applied.

Familial hemiplegic migraine

'Familial hemiplegic migraine' (FHM) is an autosomal authoritative traditional migraine subtype that characteristically contains hemiparesis (weakness of fifty per cent the body) that may final for hours, days either 7-day periods. It may be escorted by different indications, such like ataxia, state of unconsciousness and palsy.

There is scientific cover in whatever FHM cases with sporadic ataxia sort 2 and spinocerebellar ataxia sort six, gentle family childish epilepsy, and alternating hemiplegia of youth. There are 3 recognized Locus (genetics)|loci for FHM. FHM1, that accounts for about 50% of FHM cases, is triggered by alterations in a segment of DNA encoding for the P/Q-type calcium delivery method α subunit, CACNA1A. FHM1 is as well related with cerebellar deterioration. FHM2, that accounts for The foremost examination of this alteration, utilizing the bunny isoform of the delivery method communicated in oocytes, noticed that it did not change whatever calculated delivery method assets. A following outline, utilizing mortal delivery methods communicated in HEK293 Cells, noticed a not so large hyperpolarizing move in the centre for activation, a effect commonplace amid FHM1 deviants. This move outcomes in delivery methods that open at further pessimistic pissibilities and, consequently, have a developed open likelihood compared to wild-type delivery methods at nearly all pissibilities. This outline as well noticed that the R192Q distorted created nearly two times like a lot whole-cell current contrasted to wild-type delivery methods. This is not expected to a shift in sole delivery method conductance however to an equal rise in delivery method thickness. A following band perceived that this alteration is in a area essential for alteration by G protein-coupled receptors (GPCRs). GPCR activation guides to shyness of wild-type CaV2.1 flows. R192Q distorted delivery method flows are as well lessened by GPCR activation, however by a tinier quantity. A further new band has established whatever of those outcomes by generating a R192Q knockin mouse|knock-in mouse. They established that the R192Q distorted operates at further pessimistic pissibilities and that nerve cells making those delivery methods have a lot greater whole-cell current. This followed in a a lot greater quantal subject matter (the numeral of neurotransmitter packages disseminated per activity potential) and normally increased neurotransmitter discharge in R192Q airing nerve cells against wild-type. Consequently, those distorted rodents were further vulnerable to cortical-spreading-depression compared to their wild-type equivalents. The most new trials on this distorted, nevertheless, have countered whatever of those outcomes. In CaV2.1 Gene knockout|knockout nerve cells transfected with mortal delivery methods, P/Q-type flows as of distorted delivery methods are really tinier compared to their wild-type equivalent. They as well noticed a important reduce in calcium inflow throughout depolarisation, directing to lessened quantal subject matter, in distorted against wild-type airing nerve cells. Neurons airing distorted delivery methods were as well fewer capable to arbitrate repressing feed in and have tinier repressing postsynaptic flows via P/Q-type delivery methods. Further challenging with this and different deviants is needed to decide their finish influence on mortal biology.

CPSIA information can be obtained at www.ICGtesting.com
Printed in the USA
LVOW03s1931160715

446499LV00011B/399/P

9 781488 879265